The Broons

The world was introduced to The Broons family in 1936. Their black and white comic strips appeared in the new Fun Section that was part of The Sunday Post newspaper. It was seen for the first time in March of that year. They were of course a full family by that time. Maw and Paw Broon, the parents, looked after their large family of eight children. Five boys and three girls. Hen Broon was the eldest son, a very tall, beanpole of a man who tried hard without great results to charm the girls of Auchentogle. Joe his brother was a rugged, good looking sportsman. Horace was the scholar, in his final years at school and without a doubt the brains of the family. Twins, just known as Ae twin and the Ither twin were primary school aged bundles of mischief. The three girls were also very different characters. Daphne Broon was a plump, good natured lass who though she was not that good looking was never short of a boyfriend or 'click' as the Broons called them. Though all her romances were short lived she kept up her search for 'Mr Right'. Daphne's sister Maggie on the other hand was so good looking she had trouble fighting off the multitude of eligible suitors that came her way. The final daughter was simply known as 'the Bairn', a cute, curly haired bundle of joy, wise beyond her toddler years and the apple of her grandfather's eye. And what a grandfather, the legendary Granpaw Broon. A widower, Granpaw has his own cottage in Auchentogle. However he liked being part of such a large lively family and spent his time with them. Granpaw was a fly old rogue (still is) who was always on the lookout for a freebie or the chance to make some quick money.

Oor Wullie

Oor Wullie is a mischievous wee boy famed for his spiky, tousled hair and distinctive black dungarees. He met us all for the first time in 1936, in the same Sunday Post Fun Section that launched The Broons. Wullie is very much an action man and is the inspirational leader of his long standing pals, Fat Bob, Soapy Soutar and Wee Eck. On the rare occasions that Wullie sits still he parks himself on his trusty zinc bucket, a feature as old as the strip itself. Wullie's ploys and pranks often get him reported to the local policeman, the burly PC Murdoch. However there is no malice in Wullie so he and Murdoch have a sort of mutual respect. Wullie hates getting out of his bed in the mornings and hates going to bed at night. At school he drives the teacher wild by letting his mind wander far away from the lesson, although he does like PE and history – if it's about battles. After school Wullie often spends time avoiding Primrose Patterson who would like him for a boyfriend if only he didn't have grubby hands, skinned knees and a love of catching puddocks. Wullie is a huge fan of his Ma's home cooking, especially her mince and tatties with peas. His Ma and Pa get exasperated at Wullie when his adventures cause panic in their hometown of Auchenshoogle. But really they love their wild wee laddie with mischief in his eye.

Maw and Paw Broon were married in 1911, for this is their silver wedding anniversary in 1936.

Oor Wullie had a baby brother in the first years of the strip. The child disappeared after a couple of years. Probably it was too like the Bairn who appeared in The Broons.

A rare strip from 1936 where The Broons and Oor Wullie appear together.

The Broons' Family History

The material in this book's made up of the stories and tales told by word of mouth to Granpaw Broon, roond the fireside, by his auld Granny, stories that had been passed down by family fowk since the dawn o' The Broons.

Horace put them all into a book for Granpaw who was worried that with a' the new digital devices aboot, naebody was telling stories roond the fire any mair – and these historical tales would be lost forever. In honesty, some historical detail may have grown arms and legs over the centuries but through them all you will be able to recognise the humour o' Scotland's happy family.

Granpaw Broon would not let any other member of the family read the great book. Horace was sure this was because the auld rogue made the stories up as he went along.

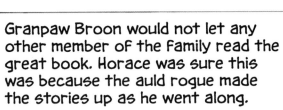

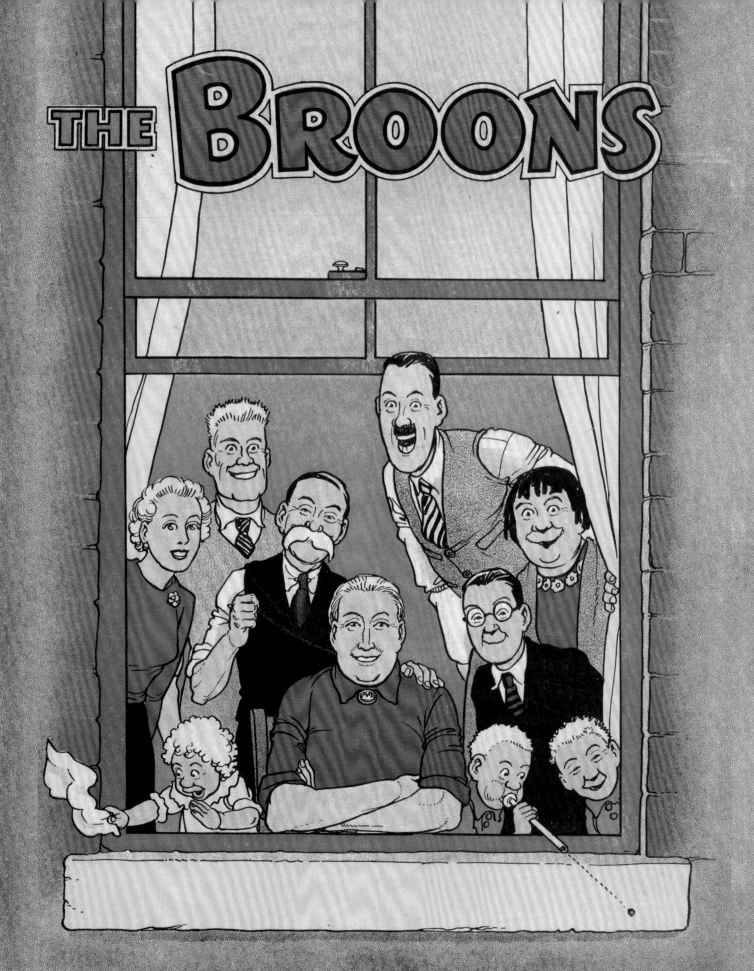

THE BROONS

Just as famous as The Broons family themselves is their address - 10 Glebe Street. A large flat in a tenement house where they have lived for 80 years.

GLEBE STREET

DUDLEY D. WATKINS

With so many people in the one house bathing caused problems.

Noise could be a problem. Sleeping arrangements were cramped.

Many storylines involved 10 Glebe Street often with the family being locked out.

Other times the family were stuck inside the house.

The tenement close walls were a message board for Daphne Broon's latest romance.
Usually the messages were drawn by the naughty Twins.

With five to a bed you have to hope
nobody snored.

Before mobile phones you just yelled up to
the window.

Early snapshots from the family album.

Many Broons and Oor Wullie strips mentioned relatives. We will show as many as we can to help build up a picture of the characters' families.

The First Broons

Information that formed the earliest stories was believed to hae come frae cave paintings and words scratched in rock at sites a' roond the world, places as far apart as Largs and Los Angeles. Granpaw is certain that this early bunnet-wearing tribe must hae been the beginning of The Broons.

Granpaw's theory was that the first humans were not Adam and Eve but were in fact Adam and Steve, the Broon brothers, gardeners in the Gairden o' Eden. Auchentogle museum did not back up this idea, but they did ask kindly if he was feeling okay. A furious Granpaw handed back his free pensioner's museum pass in protest.

Wullie Doesna Need To Sulk

He Finds " Good Things In Little Bulk."

Wullie and his little brother celebrate his birthday – but we don't know what date it was.

Wull Overdid His " New Year," It Seems.

But, Never Mind. Good Night! Sweet Dreams!

Wullie had Aunties Jessie and Bella plus Uncle Joe all living within walking distance of his house.

Maw and Paw obviously did their courting in Auchentogle.

The Broons' Auntie Lizzie lived in a house very similar to their own.

The Broons' Aunt Aggie terrifies even Granpaw.

Wullie Waited The Whole Night Through
To Find That One Plus One Made Two.

Aha! Wullie has an auntie in England – and she obviously knows what he likes.

Will Uncle Freddy be Uncle Joe's brother? Or do they just fish together?

Land Of Giants

When dinosaurs ruled the Earth men were just starting tae be menfowk you wid recognise today. They sat around playing dominoes and blethering and trying to avoid doing ony cavework. Note frae Maw Broon: This is the only bit of honesty in this whole story.

You micht wonder how man managed tae survive amongst they muckle fierce creatures. The answer is quite astounding – men at that time were huge tae, forty feet tall at least, they made the dinosaurs look tae be the size o' dugs.

But it was much worse than a thunder storm – it was the end o' the world as it was known. The end o' dinosaurs, the end o' pterodactyls, the end o' ptarmigan and certainly 'time' on the dominoes.

Thoosands and thoosands o' years later when man reappeared, he was a midget compared tae his ancestors. And the dinosaurs? They now looked mair like hieland coos.

WULLIE SHAKESPEARE

There's very little doubt, we fear —

A Broon's a Broon whatever the year!

The Broons family traits have been handed down from long ago.

The attractive couple from 1912.

A mishap during Maw and Paw's courtship. I'm sure there were many.

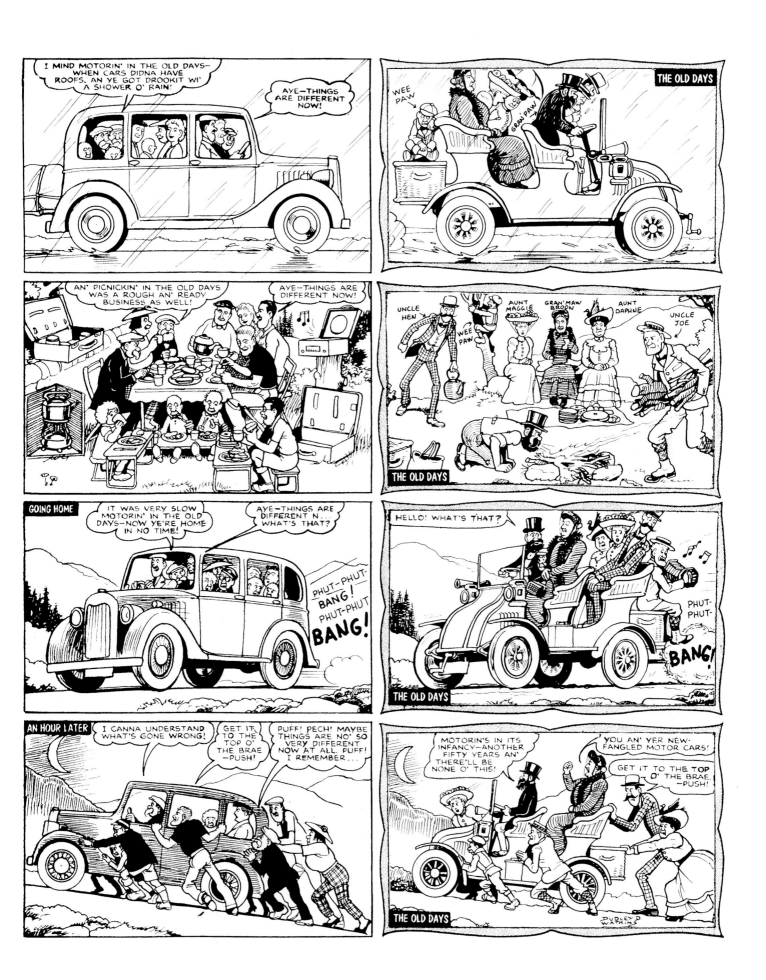

Paw Broon's family must have been well off. They had one of the first motorised cars.

A Time O' Invention

Not all prehistoric men were born equal and this was very apparent in the clan o' the cave Broons. One o' the young men was no' interested in hunting or hitting women ower the head wi' a club and dragging them hame. He was called Horace and was happiest scratching numbers and drawing on a flat stane or the cave wa'. He was sure his brain was meant tae be used for makin' great inventions.

Note Frae Maggie Broon: There's some Neanderthals in Auchentogle today that still think boppin' a lassie ower the head wi' a club and draggin' her aff is a sort o' courtship. Numpties!

Many of Horace's inventions confused the clan. His stane fitba broke a couple of taes and dented a few heids before it was thrown in the loch – and Horace along with it. But this never got him doon and great inspiration came from his mother who believed her son was destined for greatness. Every day she wid use the stane hair brush Horace had invented for her – even though she was often knocked oot doing so.

When the Second World War was declared The Broons and Oor Wullie were most patriotic. Hen and Joe Broon both enlisted and were serving infantrymen for the duration of the war.

Wullie's Uncle Watty was in the Scots Guards during the war. In this strip his name is on his kit bag - Watty Russell. Many fans think that this points to Oor Wullie's surname being Russell but it may well be that Watty is Wullie's mother's brother.

Uncle Watty or Wattie – Wullie never could spell.

Even the studious Horace was an army cadet, taught here by two brave veterans of previous wars.
Paw Broon was in the First World War and Granpaw saw service in the Boer War.

10 Glebe Street seemed to be elastic and could accommodate huge crowds.

During the war, like so many real city kids, Oor Wullie was evacuated to a country home for a time.

1945. The Broons get ready to celebrate the end of the war and the return of their heroic sons Hen and Joe.

Naked Games

CERT X (NEARLY).

Lang ago, afore onybody had heard o' Bradley Wiggins, there were Olympic games in ancient Greece. Wiggo widnae hae been able tae enter onyway 'cos there were nae bikes, just horses an' chariots. A' the runners were in the scud, aye it's hard tae believe, what wid a' the telly cameras dae if that was the case now? They widnae ken which way tae look. Maybe in ancient Greece there was an ancient credit crunch and naebody could afford claes.

Note: Few of the ancient Broons were great sportsmen, though they would take great interest in watching it and going doon the ancient bookies tae put a couple of coins on their favourite horse in the chariot race. The early Greek athletes all liked Hentos to carry the Olympic torch as he was so tall he kept it high and the sparks never got near their delicate bits.

Note from Maggie Broon. "I'd hae rather seen Sir Chris Hoy in the scud!"

BUFFALO WULLIE

SCOTLAND'S FAVOURITE - OOR WULLIE IN A BOOK

The Sunday Post 6th October 1940

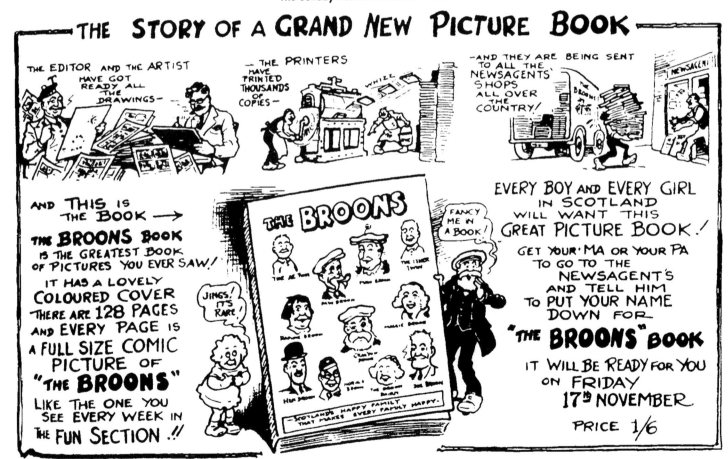

THE STORY OF A GRAND NEW PICTURE BOOK

A family history of The Broons and Oor Wullie must mention their appearances in the very successful Broons and Oor Wullie books. These annual collections are brought out every year at Christmas time, the titles alternating every year. These early adverts for the books ran in The Sunday Post newspaper and are very unusual in that the artist, Dudley D Watkins and the writer Robert D Low caricatured themselves quite accurately in the strips.

Oor Wullie 1968

Oor Wullie 1966

Oor Wullie 1962

Oor Wullie 1964

Oor Wullie 1960

Oor Wullie 1940

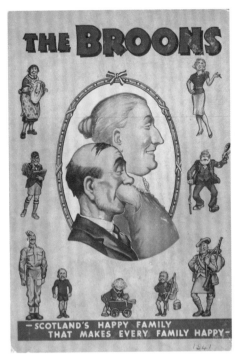

The Broons 1941

The Broons 1949

The Broons 1951

The Broons 1953

The Broons 1981

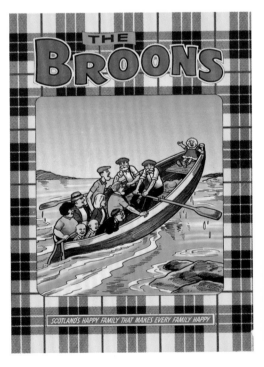

The Broons 1983

The back cover illustration from the 1962 Oor Wullie book.

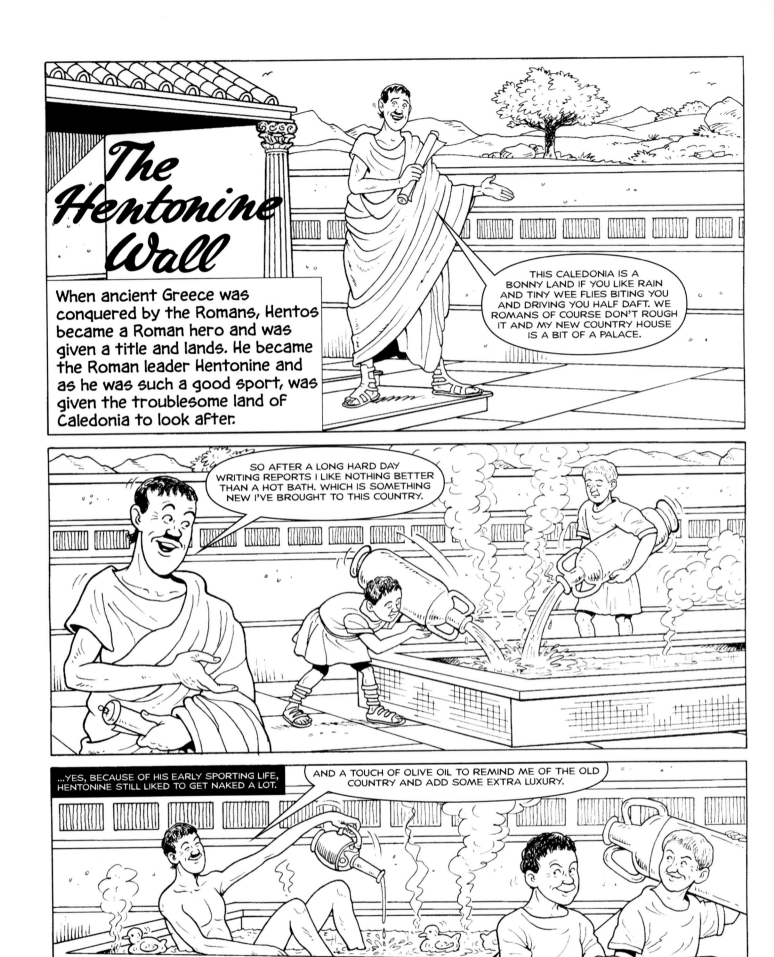

The Broons have a hideaway holiday cottage up in the Scottish Glens. It is always known as the But an' Ben. In this strip from 1943, Maw Broon sees the But an' Ben for the first time.

The whole family loved it though conditions were even more cramped than at 10 Glebe Street.

Smiles during wartime, courtesy of the But an' Ben.

A healthier lifestyle but as always funny situations occur – even in the glens.

The But an' Ben brought a new dimension to the Broons stories.

It was the Broons' holiday destination every year. Real outdoor living.

Writer RD Low was an avid outdoors man himself and spent a lot of time in a real But an' Ben.
He used it as a base for hill walking holidays.

A wartime break in the country and Daphne and Maggie are caught off guard.

Erik The Broon

Norse Sagas told o' a great Viking leader and his bold family who struck terror intae the lands they visited. He was called Erik the Broon as he never washed his sail and it was a nasty broon colour. Note frae Maw Broon: I doubt this is any ancestor o' mine.

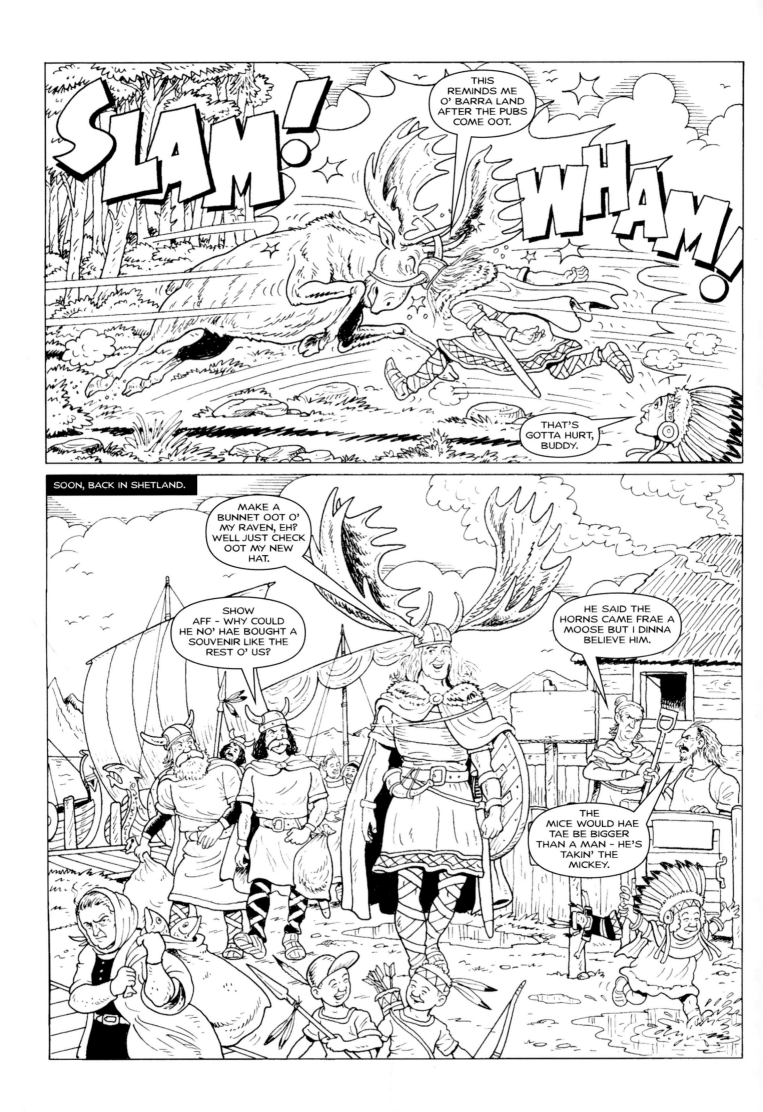

WULLIE TELL

1895 revisited for Granpaw Broon.

Wullie helps out his uncle Tam.

Are Granpaw's crimes of the past about to return and haunt him?

We learn more about Wullie – he has a cousin who lives in Edinburgh.

(Granpaw's a heavy hand wi' the spice.)

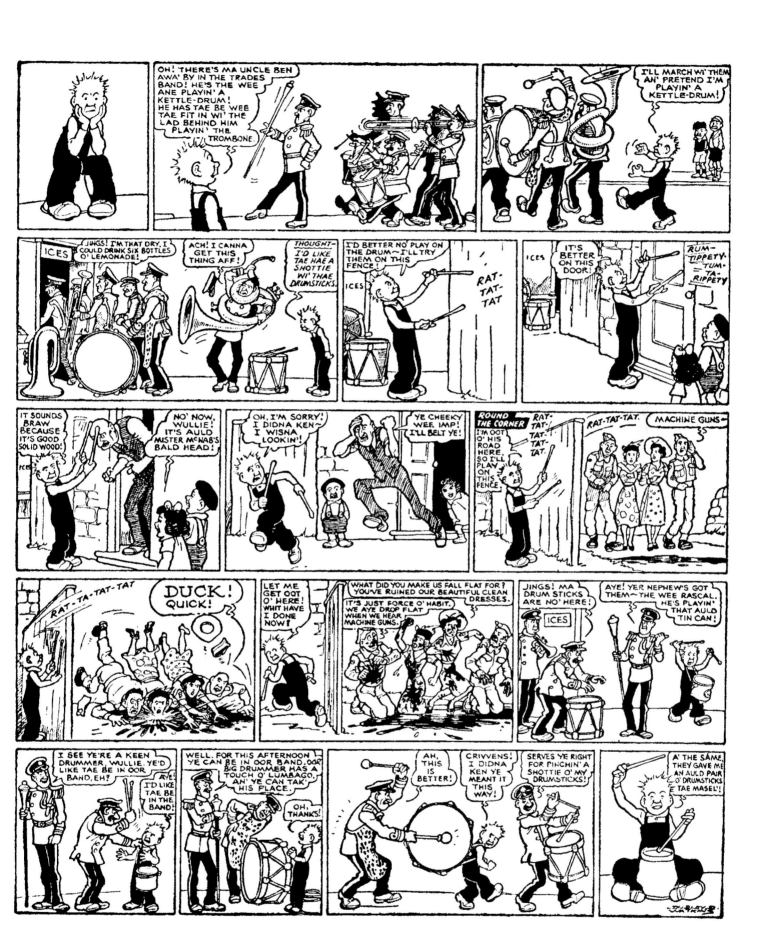

There's musical ability in Wullie's family - Uncle Ben leads the band.

A strong family resemblance. Wullie and his cousin Jim could be twins.

Good King Hen

History famously tells us that King Henry the Eighth had six wives. However, the Broons history reveals that there was a seventh wife. Little is written about her and this tale will tell you why.

The court of King Henry the Eighth is in great agitation. His seventh wife, Queen Annie of Auchterarder is about to give birth. Annie is very much hoping for a boy – some of the King's previous wives had accidents with the executioner when they failed to provide Henry with a son. Although she was in labour Queen Annie is trying to keep cool and keep her head.

Gossips at the court and the royal budgie had been tweeting for a while about the affair between the dashing lang dreep, Lord Auchentogle and her majesty Queen Annie. They had been childhood sweethearts back in Scotland until Annie had caught the King's eye when she appeared as a model on the back of early lager cans.

TO HALT A ROYAL SCANDAL, QUEEN ANNIE, THE SEVENTH WIFE, WAS WRITTEN OUT OF ALL HISTORY BY ORDER OF THE KING.

In many stories Wullie mentions Uncle Joe. He must have been a favourite.

An American side to the family – cousin Elmer is definitely from the USA.

King Robert The Broon

1314...or was it nearer quarter past one? Onyway, in the year 1314, twa nations clashed. Twa great kings determined tae dae the other doon. On one side was the dreaded English King, proud Edward the longshanks. Edward was at the head of the biggest ever English army to cross the border into Scotland. What is not commonly known is that the King was called Ted by his friends, not because it is a shortened version of Edward but because he took his teddy bear with him wherever he went. Often he would discuss battle plans with teddy. Needless to say, his battle hardened veterans were not delighted about this.

HELLO, MR TED. DO YOU THINK WE WILL WIN THE BATTLE? OH, LOOK, MEN - MR TED IS NODDING HIS HEAD.

IF THE SCOTS SEE THIS THEY'LL DIE OF LAUGHTER.

FACING KING TED ON THE SCOTTISH SIDE WAS KING ROBERT THE BROON, KNOWN TAE HIS PALS AS BOAB.

WELL, THIS IS IT - DO OR DIE THE DAY. EDWARD LONGSHANKS IS COMIN'.

LONGSHANKS INDEED - COMPARED TAE MY TALL LADS THE ENGLISH KING IS A WEE BAUCHLE.

FETCH ME A BIGGER CUDDY - THIS ANE'S OWER WEE.

...And the rest is history, as they say. A nation and a legend were born on that day. The legend tells of the farmer who helped his friend King Robert in his hour of need and was written about by Horace, the King's scribe. With the legend came a famous phrase that is used in Scotland to this day 'HELP MAH BOAB'.

Historical note: Horace the scribe was known as Spider due to his very spidery hand writing. The other legend of King Robert the Bruce getting inspired by a spider spinning its web probably originates in Spider spinning his tales.

WULLIE WORDSWORTH

Paw Broon's niece Nellie has similar looks to Maggie Broon.

It's wartime and look how many Broons can drive.

A snapshot of Maw and Paw's wedding day.

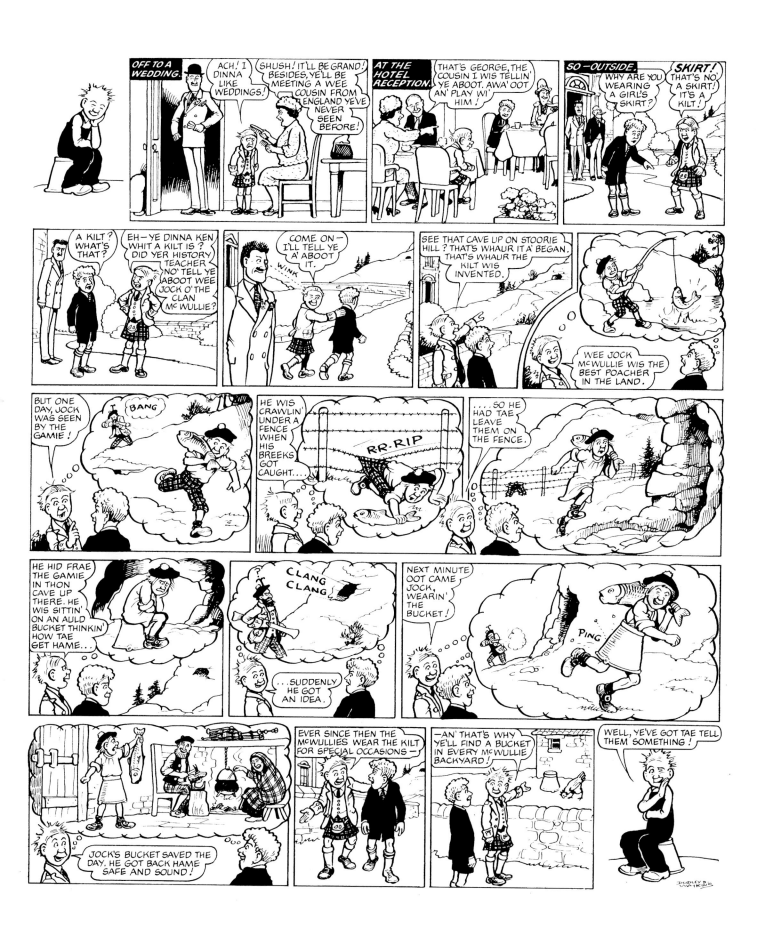

Another English cousin and he gets a lesson on Wullie-ness.

Speed Bonnie Prince

Prince Charles Edward Stuart has been on the run after defeat at Culloden in 1746. The Redcoats have been tracking him down and only the brave and loyal highlanders have made it possible for him to evade capture. Prince Charlie was considered to be a very handsome man, but unlike photographs, story tellers sometimes lie. Our tale starts in the cottage of Flora Broon, who did bed and breakfast and occasional tours over to the isles in her wee ferry boat. Now, she was a real beauty.

Sunday Post

EXCLUSIVE!

UPRISING CANCELLED DUE TO RAIN

We don't know the name of Wullie's uncle that works in the sweetie factory so let's just call him the popular one.

We can see where Maw Broon gets her statuesque looks – from her father.

A new name in the family of Wullie – McPhit.

There's an Aunt Meg living close to Wullie in Auchenshoogle.

WULLIE THE CONQUEROR

WULLIE'S ON A SCHOOL TRIP.

AT AUCHENSHOOGLE MUSEUM.

THIS IS THE BOYO TAPESTRY. IT DEPICTS THE BATTLE OF 1066 BETWEEN WILLIAM, DUKE OF NORMANDY, AND KING HAROLD.

1066:

WULLIE

hAROLD

DUKE WILLIAM? HE MUST HAE BEEN AN ANCESTOR O' MINE. BET IT'S A BRAW STORY.

PREPARE FOR BATTLE, MEN.

YES, YOUR WULLINESS.

NO' WI' EACH OTHER, YE NUMPTIES.

THE ENEMY CAMP—

PREPARE FOR BATTLE, MEN.

'MAN', YOUR HAROLDNESS. THERE'S ONLY ME.

BALANCE THAT APPLE ON YER NAPPER, TROOPER MURDOCH. I'LL SCARE THE ENEMY WI' SOME FANCY SHOOTING.

I'VE NO' LOST THE TOUCH, LADDIE. YOU CAN EAT THE APPLE FOR BEING SUCH A BRAVE BOY, MURDOCH.

BUT YOU HAVE LOST THE ARROW, SIRE, AND IT'S THE ONLY ONE WE BROUGHT.

Snapshots of what the men got up to during the war.

Maw and Paw's old pals are revealed.

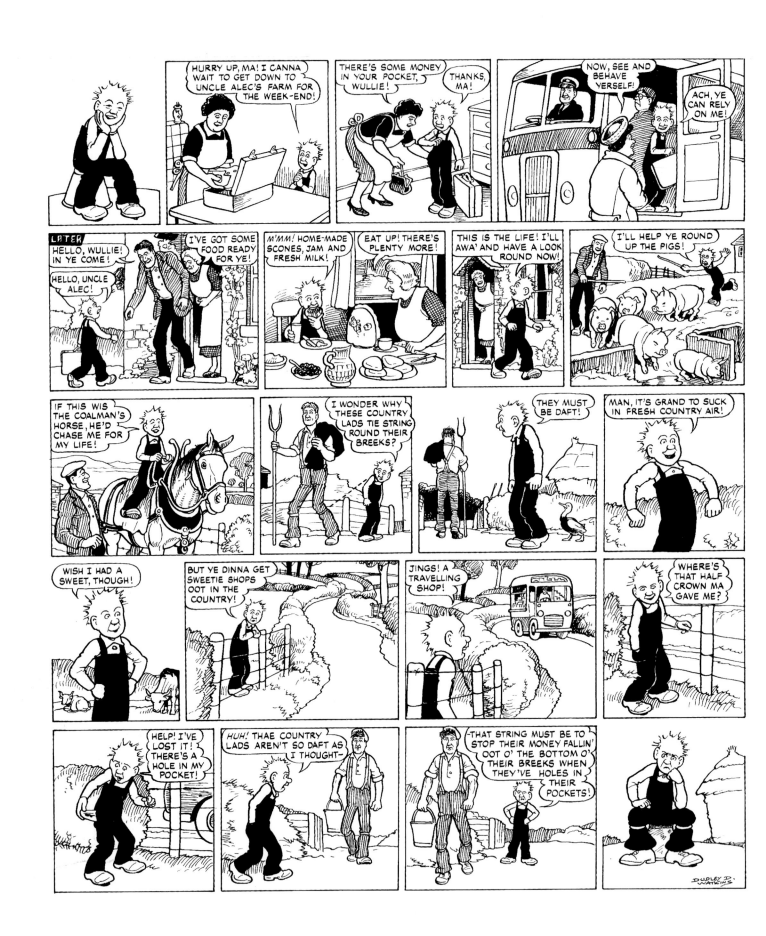

Life on Uncle Alec's farm is only a bus ride away for Wullie. The country life suits Wullie.

Auntie Jean has a tearoom at Brichty, now that's a place we've never heard of before.

Balmoral Broon

Beautiful Balmoral Castle on Deeside was a favourite retreat of Queen Victoria. She would spend long holidays enjoying the peace and tranquility of Scotland, looked after by a loyal staff that included her chamber maid, Daphne Broon and her brother Jock, the ghillie.

This day, a Wednesday, June 21st to be exact, her majesty was not amused.

SUNDAY POST

QUEEN VICTORIA EXPLODES!

What happened next was never fully reported in the press. The mystery explosion was put down to a shooting mishap, a story that Jock Broon himself told everone. Only he knew that her majesty's corsets had given way under the strain of the dumpling.

Ma has a brother in Argentina. We're getting a picture of a world wide family now.

American uncle too – and a generous one at that.

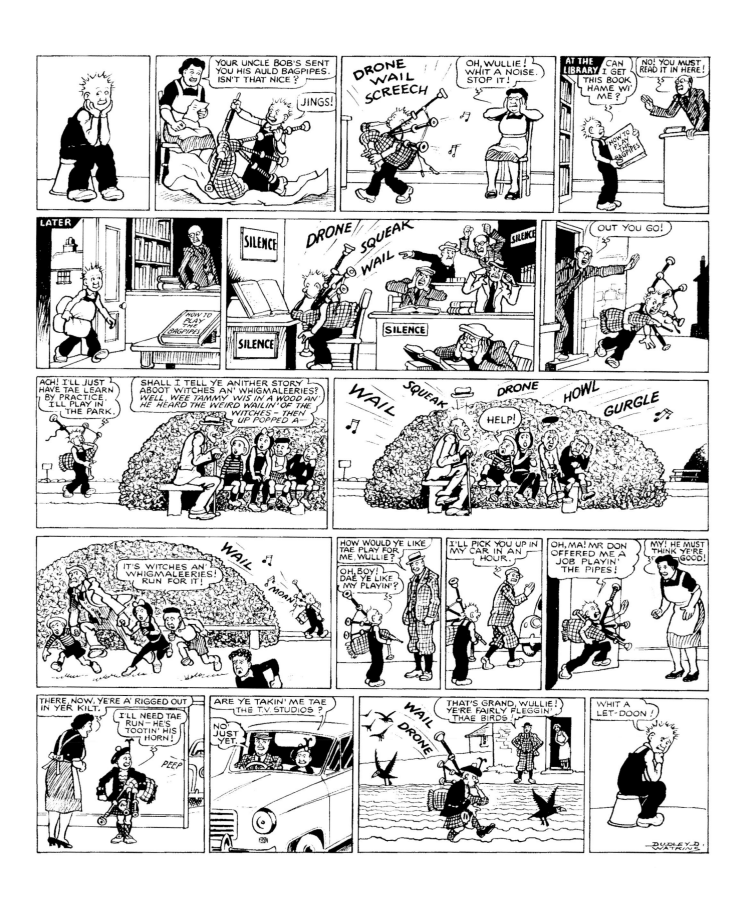

Uncle Bob sounds like a good fun guy. What a fine present to give Wullie.

Wullie reveals his ancestors – with his tongue firmly in his cheek.

Broon Of The Baltic

1912, Captain Scott's ill-fated expedition fails to reach the South Pole. Captain Scott's heroic deeds and death go down in British history for all time.

FORGOTTEN IN BRITISH HISTORY IS THE BRAVE ATTEMPT TO REACH THE NORTH POLE BY THE LITTLE KNOWN EXPLORER, BALTIC BROON. SHORT OF FUNDS, BALTIC HAD BORROWED A PLEASURE BOAT FROM OBAN PIER.

WE'RE BAITH PUFFING WELL TONIGHT, OLD GIRL.

SAUCY SUE

PUT MAIR PEATS IN THE BOILER - WE'RE NEEDING MAIR STEAM.

BALTIC'S CREW WERE IN FACT HIS FAMILY WHO HAD ALWAYS FANCIED A HOLIDAY CRUISE.

BOILER ROOM

WE'VE RUN OOT O' PEATS, CAPTAIN.

WE'VE BEEN BURNING MAIR SINCE THE WEATHER TURNED SAE CAULD.

THAT'S WHAT HAPPENS IN THE ARCTIC, YOU NUMPTIES.

PEAT

BALTIC ARRIVED HOME TO NAE FANFARES OR FANS FOR THAT MATTER. HE HAD JUST QUIETLY AND STUPIDLY FAILED. HOWEVER, LATER THAT YEAR, HE DID COME TO THE NOTICE OF THE COUNCIL.

BALTIC BROON

WULLIE WALLACE

Granpaw Broon was not averse to spinning tales about the Broon family either.

In fact the Scottish tourist board should be employing him.

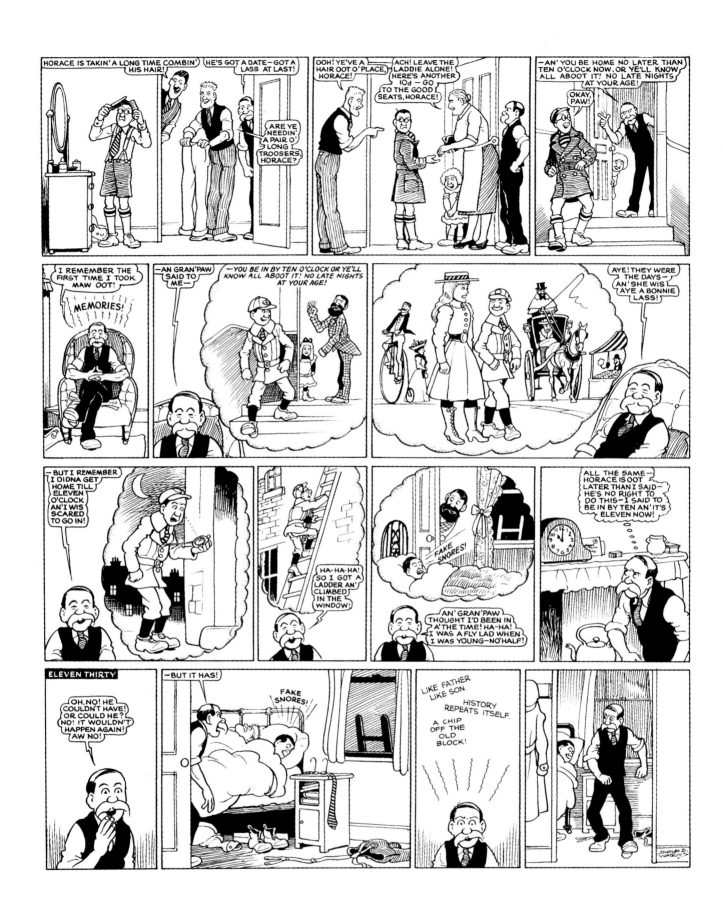

The young Paw Broon looks just like Horace.

But when his past is brought to light, Horace is much smarter.

All At Sea Wi' Maggie Broon

It's 1875 and Clyde Puffer, The Maggie, sets sail for the island of Islay from the Broomielaw pier. The Clyde Puffer was a small stumpy steam boat that delivered cargoes of all sorts to and from Glasgow and the Clyde estuary and the west coast and isles of Scotland. They were not the fastest mode of transport but provided a vital link with the remote western settlements. Cargoes varied from tons of coal to live chickens.

This year, 1875, The Maggie had a very unusual feature – a female captain. Maggie Broon was in charge and not all the crew approved.

I DINNA LIKE SAILING WI' A WUMMAN ON BOARD. WE'LL BE DOOMED, IT BRINGS BAD LUCK.

HAVERS, YOU'RE AN AULD WUMMAN YERSEL, MACPHAIL. I'D RATHER LOOK AT HER BONNY FACE THAN YOUR GREETIN' FACE ONY DAY O' THE WEEK.

BOYS – BOYS! AWA' AND MAK ME A MUG O' TEA.

JINGS! I'VE FORGOTTEN TAE PUT MY MAKE-UP ON THIS MORNING AND YE NEVER KEN WHEN I MICHT MEET A HANDSOME SAILOR.

THE MAGGIE

THE BOAT CAN LOOK AFTER ITSEL' FOR A FEW MINUTES. THERE'S ONLY ANE ROCK BETWEEN HERE AND LAGAVULIN ONYWAY.

SPIN!

POWDER

Muckle Lump was a lonely rock sitting in the western sea. It had many myths and legends attached to it. It was said that the ghostly figure of Finlay Findlater, the Phantom Fisherman, would play his bagpipes on the rock on foggy nights to warn sailors of its presence. Sailors on the Puffers swore that on the morning of January the first, the rock moved around the ocean in a zig-zag fashion. In daylight the rock was no real danger unless you were a woman driver. (Not the view of the Editor, okay. Please don't send him nasty letters.)

So the star-crossed lovers sailed into the sunset and the sea of life. Well, actually, they sailed intae Inverary and fell oot when Para gave Maggie a second-hand engagement ring he had bought frae a widow woman. As a return gift, Maggie gave Para a black eye.

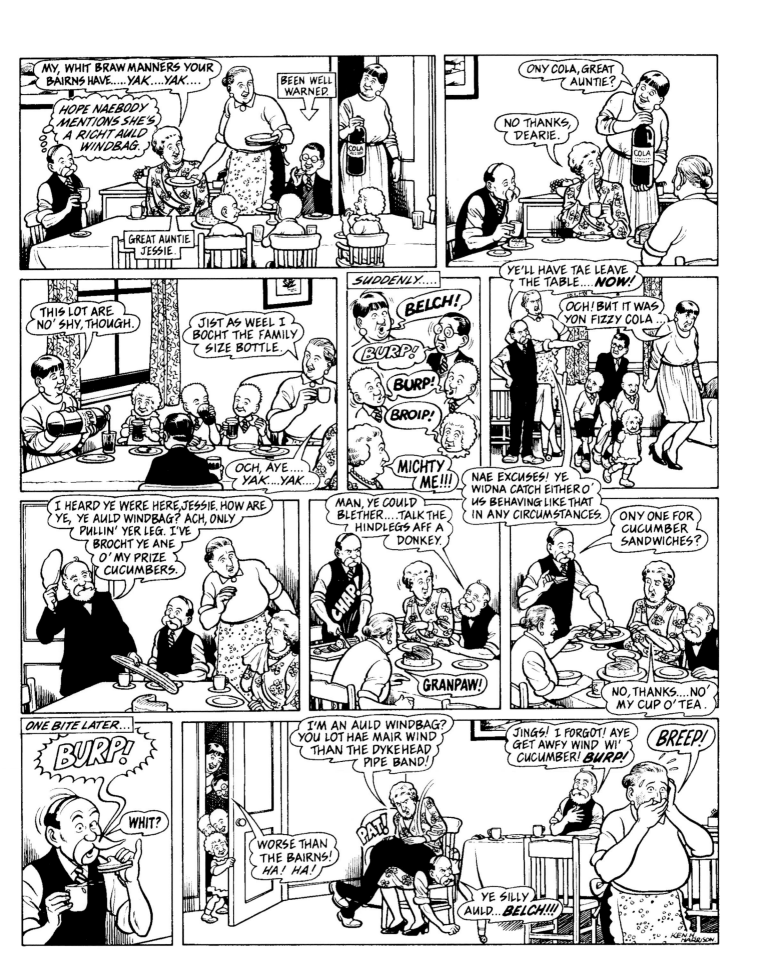

Great Aunt Jessie knows how to manhandle Paw Broon.

Another of Paw's old teachers gives us an insight about him.

Uncle Jock certainly trusts his nephew Wullie – he's given him his video camera.

There is a sect of Wullie's family from Skye – and they're Gaelic speakers.

Ma's cousin Brian is a man after Wullie's own heart.

Noah Broon's Ark

It is unclear in history whaur exactly Noah's Ark sailed frae. Somewhere in the Middle East, or Africa – even Australia. But Granpaw Broon's own studies point tae it being mair than likely somewhere aboot Glasgow - as he's never seen a place tae get so much rain. Allied tae that, Noah built a braw ship in a very short time – so the best place tae dae that would be on the Clyde. The Family laughed when they first heard him tell the story but after last year's summer holiday in Largs, they are not so sure. A week of wellies instead of bikinis, drookit ice creams and water dripping down their necks made them think again.

LAST AUGUST.

I THINK IT'S CLEARING.

YOU'VE BEEN SAYING THAT A' WEEK, PAW BROON.

THOOSANDS O' YEARS AGO.

YOU'VE BEEN SAYING THAT FOR FORTY DAYS, NOAH.

IT'S CLEARING UP.

AND THERE GOES YOUR HOOSE ROOF.

IT'S NO' A HOOSE I'M NEEDING - IT'S A BOAT.

Not a man tae waste materials Noah used the dinosaur ribs tae form the ribs o' a boat. Each day as the water rose Noah Broon worked away, he was glad tae be leaving this area as the local cave dwellers had a' objected tae him keeping a cave o' doos beside his hoose. One thing was for sure, he widnae be taking ony neighbours wi' him.

I'LL SOON KNOCK UP A BOAT AND I'LL CA' IT THE ARK.

HAMMER! HAMMER!

IT'S GUID WHAT YE'RE DOING - JUST DO IT QUICKER, MANNIE. THE WATER'S OWER MY ANKLES NOW.

I'VE ENOUGH ROOM FOR TWA ANIMALS O' EVERY SORT TAE COME WITH US.

AYE, WE'LL NEED THEM TAE BREED AND START THE WORLD A' OWER AGAIN WHEN THE WATERS GO DOON.

AND THERE'S JUST THE TWO OF US, DARLING.

WELL, NO, ACTUALLY...

Noah had been so busy building his ark that he had been neglecting his young wife, Norah, who was now sick tae death o' the auld scunner. Noah had never noticed her spending mair and mair time awa' frae the cave or that she was reading romantic tablets o' stane like there was nae tomorrow. Well, there could very well be nae tomorrow. Also, she was fed up o' Noah's untidiness, his boots were aye fu' of stane chips that he emptied oot on the flair. The romance was drowning like the world aboot them.

After this devastating news Noah used the pair of kangaroos tae jump ship when he caught sicht o' an island. This is believed tae be the start o' Australia though all records were washed away. Noah left Norah the ark if she didnae try to sue him for his pension. He also left ahint some o' his doos, one of which would help find them land and save the world.